WHAT BOOKS PRESS

AN IMPRINT OF

THE GLASS TABLE

COLLECTIVE

LOS ANGELES

ALSO BY KAREN KEVORKIAN

White Stucco Black Wing

LIZARD DREAM

KAREN KEVORKIAN

LOS ANGELES

Copyright © 2009 by Karen Kevorkian. All rights reserved. Published in the United States by What Books Press, the imprint of the Glass Table Collective, Los Angeles.

Poems in this collection appeared in their present and earlier versions in the following publications: "An Interruption" in *Quarterly West*, "Crowded Rooms" in *The Massachusetts Review*, "Speech" in *Shenandoah*, "Care of the Body" in *AGNI Online*, "She Lives and Lives" in *Hayden's Ferry Review*, "Put Down That Heavy Kettle" and "The One-Windowed Room" in *Witness*, "Willow and Pecan, Hackberry and Huisache" in *The Literary Review*, "Breath of the World" in the artists' book *the land of wandering* (University of Virgina Press, 2005), and "Eight Poems" in *Archipelago*. "Five O'Clock" and "It's Windy Now" were printed as letterpress broadsides at the Virginia Arts of the Book Center, Charlottesville, 2007-2008. I'm grateful for fellowships at the Millay Colony for the Arts in New York in 2007 and, under the beneficent auspice of Taos Mountain, at the Wurlitzer Foundation in New Mexico in 2008. Readers whose comments I valued were Gail Wronsky, Molly Bendall, Elisabeth Frost, Richard McCann, Katherine McNamara, David Lee Rubin, and, as ever, Dell Upton.

Publisher's Cataloging-In-Publication Data

Kevorkian, Karen.
  Lizard dream / Karen Kevorkian.

  p. ; cm.

  Poems in this collection have previously appeared in their present and earlier versions in other publications.
  ISBN-13: 978-0-9823542-5-4
  ISBN-10: 0-9823542-5-8

1. Poetry. I. Title.

PS3611.E96 L59 2009
811/.6   2009924553

What Books Press
23371 Mulholland Drive, no. 118
Los Angeles, CA 91364

WHATBOOKSPRESS.COM

Cover art: Gronk, *untitled*, mixed media on paper, 2009
Book design by Ashlee Goodwin, Fleuron Press.

LIZARD DREAM

for Nin

CONTENTS

An Interruption	13
Contingent Time	14
Empty Handed at 7000 Feet	15
It Being Larger Than the Category You Find Yourself In	17
Close Agreement Exists	18
A Wall Wearing Its Mask, Too	21
A Red Balloon the Size of a Tree, Heavy Breathing from the Sky	22
I Would Like to Hear It, If It Is Not Too Late	23
False Color	24
Small Emotions Are What We Recall	25
All Characters Must Find Their Ways Alone	26
Arrangement	28
Every Woman Alone Thinks She Has Got to Be a Phoenix	31
All the Conditions for Happiness	32
Speech	33
Care of the Body	34
Her House	35
Lizard Dream	36
The Face of Long Sleep	37
A One-Windowed Room	38
She Lives and Lives	39
Eurydice Mother	40
A Fall That Occurred in Recent History	41

Willow and Pecan, Hackberry and Huisache	47
How to Represent Death	48
The Dozen Crows Calling Blackly	53
Always This	54
Every Day, Insidious	55
Five O'Clock	56
Mirror Black Mirror Velvet	59
Tired of the Freeways	60
Snow White	61
The Power of Scrawl	62
I Was Not Listening	63
Crowded Rooms	64
It's Windy Now	65
Put Down That Heavy Kettle	66
Hoarse Ah-Ha	67
After a Few Pages I Understood No More Than When I Began Reading	71
Beirut May 2008	73
Baalbek May 2008	74
Emotions That Change by the Hour or Minute	75
Summer's Utmost on the East Coast	76
Last Things	78
Seeking Something at the Continent's Edge	80
A Hymn to Palm Trees	81
Life Is Mysterious as Well as Vulgar	83
Woman Talking Over a Child's Head	85
Meditation Gardens	86
Finding a Pattern in It	87

"The distance –?" I said vaguely.
"Yes, isn't it beautiful –? Just space."
"It's so intense."
"And so beyond knowing."
 The West!

    Joseph Foster, *D.H. Lawrence in Taos*

AN INTERRUPTION

A black cat appeared against a smooth adobe wall where a break
let an old cottonwood grow, a space of interruption. It was a cat

with no ears or the ears were flat and close to the head. *Here Kitty*
but it didn't come. Late November, so far the one snow
lasting a few hours

every limb and twig in a bright, white skin, emphatic tree dark
stroking the chalky field where I sit when the sun is out,
reading. The tall grass is dry now, easy to finger into yellow dust.

I never saw the black back of the cat slip into the yellow field,
metallic in the heat, the cat's black back setting off a yellow's
tinny chiming. Not lowtoned

like the throng of weathered wooden crosses
against a graveyard fence, the pueblo's custom here
of burying coffinless, the opened ground

offering years and centuries of dust. Natural then
to pull up the cross, leave a ready space,
though one has said

the appropriate things, which have come easily and
in the large sense are true,
though eyes are trained to look past

not look into other eyes. What did he know then

or what did I know. It is never possible to say that
the years that follow are worth the pain given.

CONTINGENT TIME

The cemetery with yellow trees
was scant of stones
and in many places
the earth had sunk
a body's length. Concrete slabs
for some like heavy doors.

The feel of a place
long after the event. *What
are you doing here, gringa,*
hands clasped behind your back
as if anyone would care.

EMPTY HANDED AT 7000 FEET

Wanting to say something oprahlike and boxable

don't, she said. I wrote a note but didn't send it.

Always framing
a narrative how can I sit here
and speak of nature

caught inside four walls or if walking bone cold.

No danger, said detectives

video cams at the window
for the stranger returning
for the gun that was found in the flowers.

When not rising 5000 feet into the Sangre de Cristos it is flat land here
above which clouds mass, the word *cloud* the wrong one

for vapor's dark struggle. North of the Paseo bulks the big mountain
the light fades though some days

its velvet is cobalt. Gold at a certain hour
scribbles on the rim.

The Dollar Store checkout line can be a long one. Seizing
a placemat of the bobbing *systema solar*

the ocherous bloodstreaked
yolk of fat Jupiter much larger than
moonpoor agateveined Tierra

an Anglo woman tells the cashier importantly
I'll leave my two dollars here.
Someone's waiting. You
keep the change.

Posole is carried to the table in cafes with raw onion,
red chiles, and lime for the opaque broth

microscopic fat beads in hot motion at the bowl's edge

spoon bringing up pearls of hominy,
big pork chunks tender with stiff fat cauls adhering.

Fields erupt in yellow *chamisa*, a magician opening his palm
and his bouquet of feather flowers startling. The fully loaded glock

lies in the jasmine. Walls of adobe houses, mud and straw
fluent as skin to the eye, say to the hand, *Don't touch me.*

IT BEING LARGER THAN THE CATEGORY YOU FIND YOURSELF IN

My husband left and is with this woman and he calls and says
he wants to come home but I don't know
she has some way of not letting him. I need a stone.
I heard you could help me.

I don't know. Maybe you need a bruja.

A little boy followed her around the store, a gem store
at the side of the main road going into
the small town

Long straight black hair to the waist and a Raiders black tee
hanging squarely on her body

The highway swam into the store like a hard gray river
through a wall of windows

glass shelves prismed against a glass wall
holding cut open
geodes their wide purple mouths
exploding

She bought a couple of pieces, paying
twenty-one dollars

No one else should touch them.

CLOSE AGREEMENT EXISTS
between the *Codex Fiorentino* and the *Historia de Tlaxcala* as to the omens that appeared ten years before the Spanish first came to Mexico

It seemed to bleed fire, drop by drop, like a wound in the sky.

An inkspatter of starlings,
a tremor, a sootsplat, tornado, murmuration

a clumping, a rage

the idea of black so crammed with meaning

a spread flat bedsheet's gunpowder spill,
black shot rivulets in the creases
then wild diffusion, cursive shaping

pointillist demotic on a blank folio

The temple burst into flames.

Yellow as lemons, red as a toxic sun
maroon of old leather handbags, seductively
the current invites

directed by a configuration of streambed
it swells, cold,
dark wet and rolling

taking leaves in lazy yellow moving

The people said: "The temple was struck by a blow from the sun."

Each building projected an everyday shadow
no fog softening or smoke rising from the ground

nor falling from the sky
a sickness of air

sickness of the eyes
silence of a bad sun

anything could happen
imponderable yellow ash

in places false rose or stagnant blue
nothing definite or indefinite

pointless to ask what was known
no possibility of sentiment

a hastening
like something heard

or the truth
always about to appear

> *There was a great outcry and confusion, as if the people
> shook a thousand little bells.*

Painful, like oblique light
like sidewalk ice mistaken
for broken glass

yellow caution tape's
protected space

sound of water rushing
or maybe fire

The wind lashed the water, until it boiled.

A bus door opened

everything
bagged in plastic

dogs tugging at corpses

for days, hundreds on the bridges

the bus filling with that smell
give her some air please

A weeping woman, night after night.

Soft vowels of NAFTA, maquiladoras, pistoleros,
mordidas

polychromed saviors
paper diapers

the shit. Teeth-yellow
battered grasses, beautiful

the blue Sonoran ranges
la frontera

dark star. Sore fingers
from the little thorns

her Calexico your Mexicali

her glock your AK-47, her gifts

narcotraficantes, coyotes, arroyos

A WALL WEARING ITS MASK, TOO

The house is
a little brown box
and you think
this is pleasant
the yellow leaf next to a pipe
with peeling yellow paint

Inside, adobe walls
painted white, the pale
aspen ceiling where limbs
extruded brown knots

Cordial magpie
yelling from a tree

A mud house accustomed
to those with cold fear
which politely
it ignores

Yellow leaves fluent
in the blue world

Outbursts of air
move them,
presentiments
of cold

A RED BALLOON THE SIZE OF A TREE, HEAVY BREATHING FROM THE SKY

Eventually you are old. It cannot be argued. Their

we can't cure you but I can promise you'll have no pain.
How it was to sit in the car with someone after that

thinking, she had known and my stupid ignoring.
How she'd refused what now could not be refused

a certain number of months
not years

I wouldn't advise it.

It was an industry. The stable of armchairs
beside which stood scrawny IVs from which flowed the chemicals

the if-only-I-could-eat-I-could-lick-this-thing

We eat the days. The
chew chew gobble spit. The great detachment

with which she listened to people speak of their plans.

I WOULD LIKE TO HEAR IT, IF IT IS NOT TOO LATE

I try to hear the story
careful in its settled way

the rooms I came to had
the scent of their
pink plush chairs

rain's soft assault on the roof

it is very beautiful the
green wet leaves and
dark bark each
window frames

some worm inside me
growing used to

FALSE COLOR

Hardy, this life, the dry dirt of it.
Who brings plastic flowers.
Do they fall from women's hands.
Who made the journey to Wal Mart
for wired bouquets of yellow and red,
false green leaves for the grass
that grows long and gray.
The flowers fill each fenced-in
small territory until the whole
presents a floral sea. Festive,
you think.

SMALL EMOTIONS ARE WHAT WE RECALL

It was something to squeeze in the fist
numbing coarse cold clay

a pond's surface shifting
green to brown

minnows reversing abruptly
tadpole fluff clouding bramble

dark birches punctuating the white hill

viridian the other piercings

the sky novelizing a tonality artificially blue

elements of rust
added to a polyphony deepening the story

ALL CHARACTERS MUST FIND THEIR WAYS ALONE

The glass wall of the community pool lets me think I am
stroking toward the less grand mountains to the west, the ones
gray with hard stumblings

the road away from them lined with thick groves of tall aspen
bright yellow in the cold

a small town despite the businesslike aspect
of strip malls on the Paseo del Pueblo Sur

a bright blue flotation belt strapped on
which is what I need pretending
to run through deep water.

How not to be as Emily says
confusing fear and despair

Turn pages fast to get to the amazing phrases, her

syllables of velvet
sentences of plush

A child laid to sleep in the back seat of a car. A mother's tears
as she refined her shell of *I don't care*

though the body never forgetting. Treading water then
and doing it yet

the lesson not to dive into turbulence. Eurydice wandering

Orpheus could not save her. She must be him too
in that lost place

regard herself with hot eyes. She is not Orpheus
sunset blistering the gelid water

each day light making of the mountain
something other than what it seemed the day before

ARRANGEMENT

Marfa, Texas, is not hot in December
wind thrashes the grass in the field
the ex-army base sits in, each blade
a switching lizard tail long and gray

the concrete cubes that are the art
sitting far away, almost near the road.
In the field small gray crickets
electrically hop, reflexively your shins

twitch, a vocabulary of grass
at the base of each cube and long shadows
that grow short then long again,
anything you think you see
a kind of shadow of the thing.

Yesterday a lizard came to the back balcony and warmed itself…It lay very still…
That's when I discovered the tiny eye.
It had a blackness of a different kind, the wide-awake, sober blackness of reptiles.

    Lars Gustaffson, *The Death of a Beekeeper*

someone who might become a mother, willingly or unwillingly

    Kara Walker

EVERY WOMAN ALONE THINKS SHE HAS GOT TO BE A PHOENIX

apologies to Donne

The valley is not so much
a place of hot sand
where cacti flourish
in amazing variety
though in the heat
hair smells like bread

like sleep, the gray veined
San Gabriels
rising like metal

On pale semigloss walls
long hot arrowing light

ALL THE CONDITIONS FOR HAPPINESS

The widow lived in a development's
showcase house. It was not large

you entered directly into the livingroom-diningroom
and from there into the kitchen-sittingroom

displays of hyphenation once stylish for the married

eye-level windows set high to avoid disturbing glances
from the house on the too-close lot adjoining

a sliding-glass back door framing the predictable
mounds of clouds, always flat-bottomed over the flat land
and too bright

in the yard a single sycamore, massive, not beautiful

but older than the house and still worth admiring
for its silvery peeling bark and leaves like nervous rasping hands

their whispering filling the high-windowed bedrooms at night
especially the woman's own room

when the perishing heat broke and the A/C was at last turned off.

She had the tree cut down
complaining about the leaves
the mess they made

what use was this tree the raw stump it left
smooth and ivory as a tooth.

SPEECH

A way of talking that sufficient
oo oo ah ah dull piercing thrusts

a thousand tempi
from a thousand soft gray throats
guttural mica

a whistle if a whistle were a sigh

sparrows in the heat
their vigorous *shreep shreep*

A child makes a longed-for dive
into an aquamarine pool

looking up at what divides and rejoins
on the surface

fractured secret dark

force of shadow

A widow in her house tells everything
from the beginning

>   *Well I left the house and then*

thrill in the voice
lilt as statement

querulous sheen

CARE OF THE BODY

Care of the body was sweet
besides there was nothing else.

I said are you hungry she seemed angry that she was.

If you saw what you had given years to

fish swimming on disposable placemats

you could do it
one hand tied
behind your back.

On good days we went to the Dollar Store

spill of toothbrushes, tiny porcelain dogs, red
plastic roses, bins and bins of books with blank pages

everything now she would never make good

no time to start thinking
too late for that.

Shiny bright knives of light on the sheet in the morning.

Would you like pie? It's lemon.

Why shouldn't I?

A crispness to kindness.

HER HOUSE

Her house has pale walls green as the
toxic sky and also a small clock
with a single arm and
unsynchronized
tick and tock. It's not too bad

until ten or eleven then the heat

most often we feel it
getting in and out of cars

everything is A/C, a stale icy condition
of entombment
then resurrection

though just a brief one.

OK the afternoons cool off
but by dusk the air scalds.
Oh

the sun is down

not yet.

LIZARD DREAM

A green lizard slivers on a doorframe, shaking one two
one two its wedge head
drenched cannas listing against the small stucco house

a still hawk riding pale currents
until wings raise and lower
raise and lower again

pleasure
a hawk's shadow

that comes and goes like a day of high wind
and scumbling clouds

when their quick covering
uncovering of the sun disturbs the walls of a room

and the grass labyrinths where the lizard moves

light that is there
then not there
tongue-blabbing cannas in red shock

THE FACE OF LONG SLEEP

Sun makes a hydrocarbon farewell to August gravid with wet

Gnats' madness in the streetlight penumbra

Boys' bodies on lawns succumb to sharpness of grass
that reaches up and doesn't want to let them go

Teeth rasp thunder and silence

In the road pewter sparrow feathers

A small snake's flattened interrogatory gleam

A ONE-WINDOWED ROOM

A one-windowed room of white curtains
white pillows and white sheets pulled tight

Of long-fingered blue-mapped hands
on either side of the body always done-to

that did not want food
that lifted onto the plastic chair continued to
shit and stink

the soft white cloth wrung out in warm water the
now we'll wash your face the

scarred and breastless the
it's so hot let me put some of this powder on

Mineral light on the white bed
from handsized leaves that in November
crisp and tan would fall

in March, cast off yellow spume

SHE LIVES AND LIVES

This was life. The door open
the child watching

the mother and the man rolling side to side
on the rough rug of no color

though its vague florals suggested a firmament
of honeythroated convolvulus

skinlike blooms. Hushed color. Not the gaud

of a garden catalogue where the color sloppily
spills over lines
an effect called bleeding.
She tears out

pages to save them. It's August and outside
cicadas thrum their doom song, heat

the dark doesn't quench, bare delicate
shoulders shining

from a black halter top, long dark
hair swept to one side.

EURYDICE MOTHER

I was wrapped in a blanket in her arms

my father was driving nobody was speaking

not yet dawn and we

                              rushed through
                              night's dregs

her low voice whispering

streetlights fist orange

in silvering windows our blueblack car

A FALL THAT OCCURRED IN RECENT HISTORY

Inconspicuous flowers, some cupped leaves
like bowls of spoons, the milkweed seeds'
fine tufts of silk hair the wind takes

pulpy tissue of cholla

touched stamens of the prickly pear flower
that curl and twist inward,
honeyed four o'clocks that only live at dusk

when the pure white flowers unfold

purple filaments and orange antlers,
the hawkmoths with extremely long tongues

madrone, gingko, magnolia, the sacred datura
also pure white but the margins tinged lavender

the hawkmoths stumbling from one flower to the next.
Stiff and succulent

century plants live much less than one hundred years,
bats and hummingbirds visit

the bats' bright yellow pollen stained heads.

Dusky, their fragrance, she called it.

Yawning, she chafed her well shaped hands, the palms' network
of parallelograms and grooves, crisscrossings on clay soil
after the dry spell that follows rain

rubbing her eyes she considered time

though not yet death. In her dreams his eyes were black
but she knew their true shade's dark almost reddish brown,

putting a finger to his eyelid to each corner of his mouth
as if indicating a choice of what was rarest among such beauty.
Considering the outward form

pleasure warmed her breasts and arms, her body's
inward parts, no voice naming foul, not yet *a thynge soyled
a mayde defloured*

the convolvulus furling its tissue bell. She touched her lips to it
she shook her head

absolutely still she held her breath like someone listening
then broke away
rose and sighed

put hand to unruffled hair. He was prudish and half naked.
She by glare of noon whitely dressed.

In the cool of the day they hid, damp leaves sliding around her body,
male and female, skin so warm like velvet on the bone

        now the serpent more subtil
and the small lithe lizard paused,
under his chin a red bubble inflating

a sparrow landing on a limb
and then another sparrow landing
on the first sparrow and then a sound
like bells clinking. She looked at her fingers

nails rippled like sand, little skin flags,
needlelike curlicues flung away from the bed of the nail,
pale tan spatters, wrinkled pink louverings.

Shale, limestone, dolomite, chert, shallow
marine origins of sandstone underneath
postoaks, acacias, cacti

the edwards plateau and the riogrande plain,
the hidden salt bed moving and dissolving,
a small green lizard pausing near spiky aloe
each day

hot, then wet, the soaked earth exhaling the cool,
the dank, the small, the biting, the rasp, the hard
absence that is night

as if black shapes named leaves forced themselves
against the gauze hiding it
whatever the it is

grass unstoppable, green water lapping at the wall
up which gray snails labored, air green as wet bedsheets
whose secret is *must*.

A shrieking jay appeared at the door, diving
from the coinsized leaves of the oak

a hand to protect her eyes and on the path
a still warm blue tufted small bird. She lifted it

its weight less than air. At the base of the tree
a bed of blue vinca growing. She closed the fingertip leaves
over the small body

that in her palm had been almost nothing
and only then

was the bird above silent though not too far away
a dog barked, maybe wanting water.

At the last rough dispersal the rankling grass
of the yards' waxsmelling trees, something long hidden

in all this

ugly green, the too many voices, the too much
rain talk, bird talk
car tires shushing a wet street

then a collision of air, dark chorale
she is detaching, you must let her go

a dream of lizards, birds, and bristling grass
her what if there will never be another dream

each blade at sharp angle, fierce tickle,
not *was I happy* but *what was pleasure.*

WILLOW AND PECAN,
HACKBERRY AND HUISACHE

Not a language of grief
the well rehearsed green chorus
bends to one side. A sleek blackbird erupts.

Somewhere
a chainsaw. Somewhere
a leaf blower. Somewhere

a clock ticks in a room
where doves query *one-two*
and three hah hah over there
collect
a pear go comb
your hair go say
a prayer oh don't
be scared opulent

pink flames at the window
western sky graying

shadow wants the streets

still body on the bed. Dove lusters
Go now.

Oh oh oh from the trees.

HOW TO REPRESENT DEATH

Benaki Museum, Athens

A woman withdraws toward
the perimeter of the stele
raising her shawl
she is covering her head
maybe all of her body

to avoid the touch of
those whom she leaves

whose hands nevertheless
are reaching
she will not let them
touch her
not even the ones at her feet
the child or the little dog

because the dead have no more wish to be
used by us they are finished

Roman Agora, Athens

Foundation stones like teeth
loose in a jaw
bitch with long teats trying to
shake off the dusty puppy
that hangs on

small votive figures lacking
well defined features
next to the molds that formed them
the inverted selves

Which is most true
the second guess

or lack of shadow beneath
the sun at its zenith

The blowing wind or a figure cloaked
in flowing stone

So shadows are red?

    Lars Gustafsson, "Theory of Colors"

THE DOZEN CROWS CALLING BLACKLY

Pale bodied woman at the window
of a brick house that rouges
a pale morning. Come back to bed

from the unwound sheets. Only what's observed

black crow caw not a dog's bark

black diagonal echo

unwinding peel
knife paring

seeking pith

every morning, gray squirrel shooting
down a wet limb

every morning the slide down,
higher now

sun scalding
corner of the eye.

ALWAYS THIS

Always this going faster
in the chest. Implacable

red orange of brick as the
white gutters and window frames

depict a house. Leaf rust
doesn't let go. Thickets

erupting green

the feeling that wants escape,
something slower

blue.

EVERY DAY, INSIDIOUS

Every day, insidious pleasure

leaves touching

little sighs

and thinking this won't last and wanting to seize

and then

to seize becomes foreign as if the leaves
spoke Etruscan some excess

of vowel sounds or Cantonese.

FIVE O'CLOCK

Talking Texan, I'm told my speech
on the phone becomes incomprehensible

explaining that white lights strung around
palm tree trunks please me

that every day at 5:15 birds come,
first in small groups then their veil flung

around the bowl of the yard
with a motion that is final and dark.

How do you know they are the same ones
every day. I don't.

It's as if they say we draw it to a close

don't imagine
we won't. At 5:30 coral blunders

against night. Then the masquerade

the roiling ceiling's
baroque clouds, more cold

behind this dainty blue.

Does the snow mean visits from birds
will be over

then monochrome
the day?

Being human
loving owning.

The newspaper says this is how it is

this is who you are.

Wind and its lunatic *ow ow*.

What's about to change?
The face leaning into the watery
mirror's imprison?

Heart flying from the mouth
at a door's petulant thwock?

Man in the room
talking on the phone.

Radio skirls
a single bird punctuates
pen scrapes paper.

Cars on the road
here's another car

every day counting

another one gone.

Sun a little lower now
shadow muddying the yard

the body writing in

its final heat. Oh
shadow.

Dark brush of the arm.

MIRROR BLACK MIRROR VELVET

Mirror black mirror velvet

you and your secrets
the message written backwards

it's one way to tell them

and when it cracks

better not
let breath silver the face

and how did he and how did I

trust the sheen

TIRED OF THE FREEWAYS

Plunge
from the offramp
to the trough of the road, the day vaporous

with mesquite feathers and the stillness
of solid fire,
standing on an old

oddly angled mound
looking out
across the live oaks that canopy
streets' diffused shadows

low spreading, and some pecan

drifting in what I can't call
indifferent memory

gelatinous daylight
in the distance and dark arising.

SNOW WHITE

Snow inscribes the trees' clinging

white *give to me such kisses*

acts of recall. Interceptions

now he kneels to kiss

the sleeping body imperfect

pages. No hurry now. Falling

the pewter blade speeds the dark

not necessity *not goading*

sunrise, red leaves reckoning

not waking but dreaming.

THE POWER OF SCRAWL

The orange cat is always sleeping now,
under his chin a new knot
and one under his right ear

every morning, the front door opening

he looks out

sun bleeding onto the porch,
feet sparkling, the power of scrawl.
We wash ourselves

in red light. A truck passes
seismically. The cat

cannot see, at the truck's thunder
jerks his blind face upright.

Every morning overhead

dragging shoes. Anchor.
Then
no. Don't

ask the question
if you won't like the answer.

I WAS NOT LISTENING

I was not listening I was remembering small lights strung in the dark
by a narrow river

reflections like fireflies ricocheting off smooth water that was both
brown and green

like a mirror in a dark room that the headlights of turning cars
ply with light

the shivering of my yellow skirt in warm, still air

whatever it was I was waiting for. How palm fronds and banana leaves

shone slickly like swords. She was remembering when not yet twenty
she lost her job and her tears and her brother saying *go dress up*

taking her to a hotel roof garden where a dance band played
and there was a little breeze

a paste of talcum between her breasts and her thighs, an ice cube
she ran across her throat, across the back of her neck.

CROWDED ROOMS

Flying in over blue
beanshaped backyard pools
and saying I lived there
and there near the medicinal
eucalyptus the gamey
secret of the whiteconed
datura whose tissue cup
I lifted and there
it would be rankly sweet
in a starving time.
On hot days
her leather car seat
breathed her perfumes
one called youth dew
and the other called
happy. In Birmingham
the aged very dark woman
in elegant lavender whose
thin legs were gray as
tree bark if tree bark were
sheathed in nylon mauve
and transparent
she had that smell too.
I never asked all the
bristly stuff. Warring
shadows soft abrasions.
My adult voice.
My any minute now.
All those green explosions
slaps of light
opening the car door.

IT'S WINDY NOW

A river of force through the trees

put the stone in your pocket
let it take you

*dearest no one could have been
a better* blue surveillance

turkey buzzards
22 days until equinox

squirrels flirt on a powerline
noon's gray explosions.

If you lost all *sectarian violence*
would you disappear

into your own embrace? Would you
hear the river?

PUT DOWN THAT HEAVY KETTLE

Put down the heavy kettle I was not
a good mother I was a
good mother a little bit

pequeño pequeñito
pequeñissimo

a glass of wine

it's after midnight just one the usual

swearing swearing
swearing

I was not a good mother I was

a good mother the tide moves
in the trees someone watches

from a window someone
who should get out

HOARSE AH-HA

Hoarse ah-ha of the carcass-picking crow threads the corridor

of levitating pink petals, the lyric life admiring the discontinuous,

perfume of a suburban spring, the cut grass fried-onion acrid,

but what of the killings? Pink petals shower a brick house,

then another, then again. Because it is spring,

grass nourished to a neon screech, star-fingered leaves

of a japanese maple floating dried blood dark in their newness,

someone comes to mow the grass, someone comes to clean.

Day is long
The night will pass
With or without the rain
We need so badly

    C.D. Wright, "Body Language"

AFTER A FEW PAGES I UNDERSTOOD NO MORE THAN WHEN I BEGAN READING

He was watching *The Battle of Algiers*, which he said
was just like today. An Algerian angry with the French joined a group,
then the French burned down a building, many dying.

The end showing a general like Rumsfeld saying
it was finished now and
someone else saying no it wasn't.

She told him how she felt, which wasn't purposeful or
decisive. Why could she not care? In bed

she read letters written by Pliny the Younger about
the eruption of Vesuvius and the covering of Pompeii
and Herculaneum with 30 meters of hot rock.

Although the earth shook, Pliny said, *I am not sure
whether I should call it brave or foolish,* but
he asked for a book and read it as if for pleasure

even continuing to write out what he had started on.
Then came a friend of my uncle's

*when he saw my mother and me sitting there, and me
even reading, he rebuked my mother for putting up
with me and me for my lack of concern. Nevertheless*

I remained buried in my book. Pliny's uncle, having hurried
to the place the others were fleeing, then went to bed
and actually fell asleep. *But the courtyard that his bedroom
gave onto was now filling up with ashes mixed with pumice*

so if he stayed in the bedroom any longer
he would not be able to get out. Awakened
he discussed what was happening. Should he

remain indoors or wander in the open
for the building was rocking with frequent and severe tremors
and seemed to be swaying back and forth as if shaken
from its foundation. His uncle left at last, though

when daylight came his body was found, intact, uninjured,
Covered and dressed just as he had been,
more like someone asleep than dead.

BEIRUT MAY 2008

Assembling what was known in the fever glitter of what was not known

the vocabulary of acronyms, bonjours and mercis elided
into Arabic. I had not been the one in the room

above Hamra Street, looking down on the man in the shrubs
rocket launcher on his shoulder. I did not know the
shrapnel in the wall

I could leave it, a souvenir

who was and was not fighting whom that week. I drove past the Green Line,
the Holiday Inn's half-eaten tower

*they talk of leaving it this way, a monument. Believe me
since the bombing downtown has been dead*

Drug wars I told them *though not where I live.*

BAALBEK MAY 2008

Women bending over in fields near patched coarse-cloth shelters
Iraqis, they are stateless

Posters of Arafat on one side of the road
the Palestinian side

Amplified voice of the muezzin caroming off stone
gunfire's falsetto ping not too far away,
a celebration

2000-year-old columns broken on the ground
carved lion heads as tall as one man
standing on another's shoulders

Rides for sale on a pale furred camel with calloused swollen knees

Picture, the owner said

EMOTIONS THAT CHANGE BY THE HOUR OR MINUTE

Feeling happy? Because of what I felt in the dream?
A body at ease on the bed, the escape I'd made

covered to my ankles in my black coat
from the place even colder than this one

where I'd learned with my senses
what I'd only imagined? Outside the snow

pleasantly shushes orange roofs
with a quiet that isn't, sibilant intimacy

of shrill falling. In the community pool a woman
cradles a man whose legs can only dangle

his face a cameo of intelligence and calm
in the gush of blue, outside the snow languishing

with the regularity of a looped film's white spatter

hissing like my dream that desire takes
whatever it can, as prettily as light

teasing moiré designs on shapeshifting water

SUMMER'S UTMOST ON THE EAST COAST

Black chantilly tree limbs scratch
a bedsheet sky, the roachsize hummer

teases a frou of pink crepe,
distant trucks shuddering, redbud

pods pendant, in one month
they will brown, oh the waiting

old ditherer, second guesser,
like rain worrying the hedge

pull out that portmanteau
nature vocab, antique skidalong

of self, find ice sheer enough
to crack at a palm swat.

On the other coast it never rains
but for a few days then only

sunfogsmogsunfog

sometimes dense as rain, ice
shavings, equivocation

you get used to, wet that neither
drenches nor thuds

but gusts the way a bride
after toasts will bunch

her long skirt for dancing
brightness without heat.

On this coast the end of August is very hot,
leaves stop breathing then

the rains come, wet sits on
drying leaves, no more exhale

insects gaining shrill static force
electrifying afternoons, finally crying

darkness, come, wetness

reaching inside the house
where walls thrum, floorboards quiver

and the doom song feels its way
igniting silence in the slipping-away

slow-engulfing hour
where you turn in double darkness

receptive in the expectant night
cicadas dithyrambing until high vibrations

crucify the uppermost, the oratorios.

LAST THINGS

1
Lilacs five ninety five a stem in late April, bucketed,
cloudlike at the flower shop door

Dark green plastic bags lolling with a shaved lawn's clippings

and their way here of rendering bushes geometrically,
balls of green tufting juniper, hibiscus shrubs cubed

Stray on the grass a fuschia saucersized bloom

Wizened palm fronds fallen in the street
from a distance carcasslike

all so lovely here

2
Why say something, fog, for instance, is like a shroud
when it is a plastic string like the one binding the newspaper
landing on the doorstep finally binding the jaw

Through a closed window the silent hitherthithering
of palm fronds resembles the feel of water
shudderfeathering against legs. Offstage a fanfare

sheets of metal's thunderous rattling. Spinal
shadows of fire escapes on late day's luminous walls

On zigzag waves, zircon dancing

3
In front of the auto muffler store
the St. Vitus frenzy of the Inflatable Man

air currents electrifying balloon arms that erupt
in the air hooray!
so helpless

he is at the mercy of whomever
has a finger on the pump

steady, the painted smile

despite the random jets stiffening
his arms into help! I give up!

4
At night through open windows a loose heat
of orange blossom and cum cries
spreads like a dropped stone's

circles on water still as sand

oh and oh and oh and oh
close the window now

SEEKING SOMETHING AT THE CONTINENT'S EDGE

A woman up to her knees in the surf
raises a garland of kelp
swings it slowly. When we first came to this city

many fathers seemed to be killing their children

now gangs shoot anyone incorrectly
answering the question

Where are you from

Child on his stomach in the shallow water
reaches toward shore
wanting to be taken by a force of ebbing

better he does not see it coming

pleasure
at a sudden helpless feeling

A surfer waiting for a wave to ride him

slides ashore, peels halfway down
his shining

wetsuit, the long prehensile
zipper tail wigwagging

A HYMN TO PALM TREES

They are transplants and there are those
who because of their not being native
would rid the sky
of their punctuation

their leaning-into offshore wind
rather than letting it push them away from
incalculable blue

I am so happy when taking a curve, especially
on the coastal veering highway,

my weight against the centrifugal tug
from the perimeter, resisting the center

the choppy sea with its bright exclamations,
little hot shadows on the cold.

I could keep doing this

like the tall skinny palms with whom I share
the stranger's sensibility. Wind from the ocean
tries to make them lie down

but palms understand what it is to resist
and row diligently down 4th, 5th, and 6th streets
with thinness, fineness, delicacy

attributes rarely praised,
perforating the air like biting.

Unlike ordinary dithering trees they are stick forms
that offer no more than the distraction

of their goofy green hats,
a probability of not falling.

LIFE IS MYSTERIOUS AS WELL AS VULGAR

Like a cat chasing nothing at all
hair smokes a gamey unwashed that says you're alive

A store named Drugtown, maybe it's a joke

the cheek kiss your long flowing and the man's
sheer bamboo it's organic

every wrist's fat wooden
meditation beads
sliding on elasticized cord

icicle shadows lengthening to black arrows
ever more poignant

where does the story end

where the sea shines mostly, shivering
aluminum

Why does the to-and-froing of palm tree foliage
after all just another form
of random movement

seem a pleasure,
its paper-spinning-off-the-press tunes

a squirrel's tail languid as a bridesmaid fanning
her taffeta skirt outside a church,
claws sqrittching

the girls possess solid muscular bodies
and smooth arms

flipping open their phones and nasally helloing
they study the small screens

the coastline curving like a body lying on its side

lifted arm cushioning
the head that is Malibu

spangled the space the body curves around

WOMAN TALKING OVER A CHILD'S HEAD

Put me in a hospital

the child's deliberate crayon stroking, hard pressed
opaque blue, shining.

Bright hot chrome of rickrack waves serially repeating

scrape of metal on cement, a table moved to the shade.

Squinting, you think you see a pattern. The sun,
that godlet

finally lays down its metal shield. I don't know
what to say about the child.

MEDITATION GARDENS

A conflagration of carp
thick lips gasping
for cat food oblivious
to the one swan
darkly still
overhead. Flickering
turtles' mossy plates
the red and yellow
carp thump aside.

FINDING A PATTERN IN IT

1
If the cactus has only one main trunk at ground level
the old man sitting upright and sweating on his sofa
is a saguaro if a number of stems at ground level
a son at one end and the other son in the chair

turn to page twenty-one. On the mute television
a tank on the road. If the stems have nine ribs or less
it is a senita. Then some city streets where angrily
ten or more gather an organ pipe cactus
the streamer beneath in Arabic moving right to left.

If the main central spine is round at the base and not twisted
the children shout in the hall with their games. If the other spines
are not very long turn to page twenty-six *don't you wish to lie down.*

If the fruits are dry and have long spines if the fruits are flesh
and have no spines if the stems are reddish or bluish green
if the top is flattened or depressed if it is not *not yet.*

2
Might there not be a sublime point of balance
if the hoods on the ends of the central spines
are one-twelfth inch in diameter a fine
neutrality that place that refuses to disbelieve

if the hooks are one-sixteenth inch distant across
then everything is contingent. If the radial spines
are very rigid and stout if some are flexible.

Those who believe it will sort itself out eventually

or it will be sorted out. If the main central spine is not
hooked like a fishhook or if it is. Whether the verb
is active or passive is important and slippery.

3
A fist of people gathered on the ready earth.
This is the life the wife said. And after
the large man and the small man and the man
wearing the blue shirt that here was the uniform

using only muscles lowered it until it was
out of sight, the blue shirted worker flung
the webbing straps with a gesture so impatient
and final, the straps coiling uncoiling in the air

shivering into a heap near the brown dirt pile
the grayed plastic grass almost covered
wind having lifted one corner

This is the life you would say having a good time.
This is the life meaning the short dream.

Far enough away that other dark clothed figures
were indistinguishably small but nevertheless
could be seen not leaving but staying
while a little earth moving machine

began to push dirt, batter it, ram it
the singing metal unsettling in its reach
then a priest in an embroidered robe raised a brass bowl
wind coiling uncoiling gray smoke.

WORKS REFERRED TO

Joseph Foster, *D.H. Lawrence in Taos* (University of New Mexico Press, 1972), an effusive memoir.

From exhibition signage for *Kara Walker: My Complement, My Enemy, My Oppressor, My Love*, Hammer Museum, Los Angeles, March 2 – June 8, 2008.

"Every Man Alone Thinks He Has Got to Be a Phoenix" is the title of John Donne's poem.

"Arrangement" refers to the Chinati Foundation's outdoor site in Marfa, Texas, which exhibits the large geometric forms by sculptor Donald Judd (1928-1994).

"Close Agreement Exists" owes to Miguel Leon-Portilla, ed., *The Broken Spears: The Aztec Account of the Conquest of Mexico*, trans. Angel Maria Garibay K. and Lysander Kemp (Beacon Press, 1982), which translates documents from the Nahuatl that describe omens related to the consequences of the sixteenth-century arrival of the Spanish in Mexico.

"Theory of Colors" by Lars Gustafsson is from *The Road to Xanadu* (Copper Canyon Press, 2008), a book of poems. *The Death of a Beekeeper*, trans. J.K. Swaffar and G.H. Weber (New Directions, 1981), is a novel by Gustafsson, who is a Swedish poet, fiction writer, and philosopher.

"Body Language," by C.D. Wright, is from *One Big Self: An Investigation* (Copper Canyon Press, 2007), a book of poems.

"After a Few Pages I Understood No More Than When I Began Reading" quotes from Benedicte Gilman, trans., *Ashen Sky: The Letters of Pliny the Younger on the Eruption of Vesuvius* (The J. Paul Getty Museum, 2007). *The Battle of Algiers*, dir. Gillo Pontecorvo (1965), dramatizes the Algerian uprising against French troops occupying their country.

KAREN KEVORKIAN has published *White Stucco Black Wing* (Red Hen Press, 2004) and poetry and fiction in journals including *Antioch Review, AGNI, Fiction International, Five Fingers Review, Los Angeles Review, Massachusetts Review, Mississippi Review, Shenandoah,* and *VOLT;* and in online chapbooks for *Archipelago* and *The Drunken Boat;* and in the anthologies *the land of wandering* (University of Virginia Press, 2005) and *Line Drives* (Southern Illinois Press, 2002). Now teaching in the English department at the University of California at Los Angeles, recently she was a member of the creative writing faculty at the University of Virginia. She has received fellowships from the Djerassi, Ucross, and Wurlitzer foundations and the Millay and MacDowell colonies. Born in San Antonio, she lives in Culver City, California.

www.ingramcontent.com/pod-product-compliance
Lightning Source LLC
Chambersburg PA
CBHW031300290426
44109CB00012B/659